AF473927

INTERIOR PATTERNS

Wallpaper, Furnishings & Home Decor

INTERIOR PATTERNS — **Wallpaper, Furnishings & Home Decor**

EDITED & PUBLISHED BY SendPoints Publishing Co., Ltd.
PUBLISHER: Lin Gengli
PUBLISHING DIRECTOR: Lin Shijian
EDITORIAL DIRECTOR: Sundae Li
EXECUTIVE EDITOR: Coco Xian, Ellyse Ho
ART DIRECTOR: He Wanling
EXECUTIVE ART EDITOR: Peng Lingbo
PROOFREADING: Sundae Li

ADDRESS: Room 15A Block 9 Tsui Chuk Garden, Wong Tai Sin, Kowloon, Hong Kong
TEL: +852-35832323 / **FAX:** +852-35832448
EMAIL: info@sendpoints.cn

DISTRIBUTED BY Guangzhou SendPoints Book Co., Ltd.
SALES MANAGER: Zhang Juan (China), Sissi (International)
GUANGZHOU: +86-20-89095121
BEIJING: +86-10-84139071
SHANGHAI: +86-21-63523469
EMAIL: overseas01@sendpoints.cn
WEBSITE: www.sendpoints.cn

ISBN 978-988-13835-5-6

Printed and bound in China

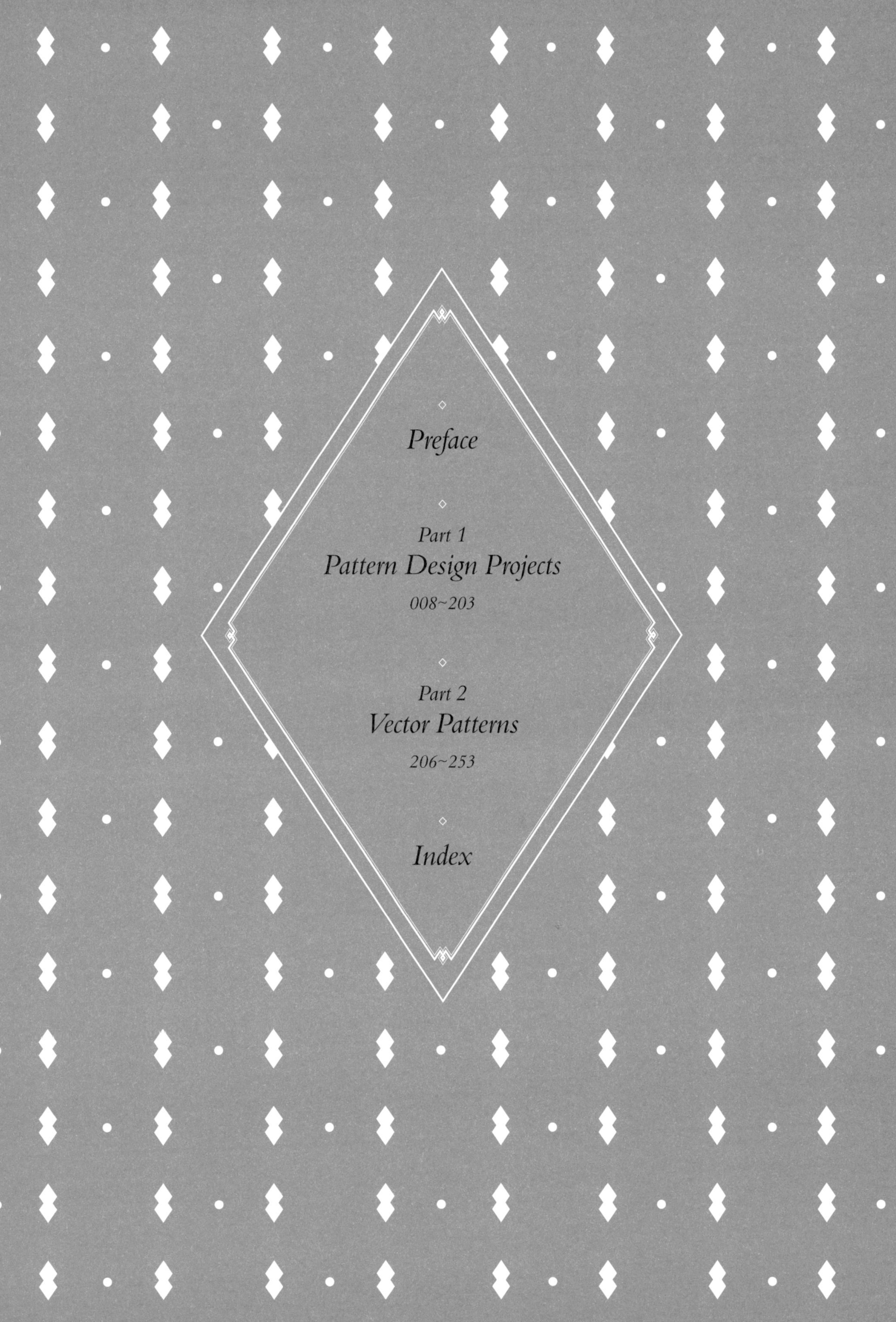

PREFACE

BY Katie Leede

I just returned from India, a country where no two saris are alike. Women walk to the markets pulsating in swaths of richly toned cottons and silks with their intricate patterns of pearls held in place by metallic threads glinting in the sun. The palpable joy with which these women adorn themselves in cloth took my breath away. The display of color and pattern was Nirvana to me.

When I was young, my mother used to dress me in bold, bright dresses from Marimekko, a Finnish company renowned for its original prints. We lived in a white, modern house with shutters used for privacy. Except in the dining room where the drapes were made of precious silk velvet the color of crushed crimson. I remember being encouraged to look at them shimmer. My favorite activity was playing with my dollhouse. I often re-painted the rooms, reworked the furniture layout, and used scraps of old fabric for curtains. Looking back, I see that my passion for textiles was sparked by the comfort and pleasure I took in my childhood from the look and feel of fabrics on my skin, in our home, and in the imaginative world of my dollhouse.

Decorating came easily for me. Nothing thrilled me more than to spend hours pondering over which fabrics and carpets to choose. Soon my curiosity led me to incorporate rare, antique textiles into my design schemes. I repurposed them on headboards, ottomans, pillows, and sofas. I understood that cultural soul lived on in these fabrics, infusing my interiors with a subtle, emotional patina that was hard to put your finger on but made for extraordinary beauty nonetheless. My husband and I were simultaneously in the habit of traveling with our young children to far flung places like Bali and, yes, China, so I had the added delight of going on treasure hunts for unique finds like the delicately embroidered wedding shawl I picked up one summer in Crete.

I believe interior design is so much more than just aesthetics. It's about achieving comfort, making spaces work for us so we lead happier, more productive lives and let us not forget the prestige that attends a harmoniously decorated home. And, of course, pattern is the most evocative of all decorating tools as the patterns we personally choose to incorporate into our living spaces powerfully and simultaneously communicate who we are behind closed doors and how we wish to be perceived by the outside world. Patterns do much of the heavy lifting in any interior. They unify the color scheme and bring together many colors, help highlight architectural features and define separate areas, and transport us to different states of mind depending on the scale and design. What I love most about using pattern however is that you can experiment with them, try them out and see what suits best for now. And then there are the tricks of the trade! Work with an odd number of prints for the most harmonious results. Vary the scale: one large, one medium, and one small pattern per room works best. Allow your boldest pattern in a room to be the star and be sure it incorporates all the colors of the overall design scheme. Let the other patterns play quieter, more supporting roles. Then watch how patterns make a room sing.

I was honored to be asked to be part of this book celebrating what I adore. I find the community of those who worship at the alter of pattern, color and design to be some of the most generous of spirit people I know. I count myself blessed to be part of this global family that is united in our gratitude for the boundless creativity on display everywhere we look and by our devotion to crafts that give expression to this joy we share. I encourage you to allow the images in this book to ignite your own desire to join in the journey of using color and pattern in your own home.

Katie Leede

Part 1

Pattern Design Projects

008~203

Spain

Little Red Riding Hood

DESIGNER: Catalina Estrada

catalinaestrada.com

Spain

Princes Garden

DESIGNER: Catalina Estrada

catalinaestrada.com

GRAPHIC STYLE
THINGS I HAVE LEARNED

Spain

Life Tree

DESIGNER: Catalina Estrada

catalinaestrada.com

Hummingbirds

DESIGNER: Catalina Estrada

catalinaestrada.com

Spain

Wallpaper Collection Patterns

DESIGNER: Catalina Estrada

catalinaestrada.com

catalinaestrada.com

Owl Forest

catalinaestrada.com

Pantheon

DESIGNER: Studio Job

www.studiojob.be

Belgium / The Netherlands
Alt Deutsch
DESIGNER: Studio Job
www.studiojob.be

Industry

DESIGNER: Studio Job

www.studiojob.be

l'Afrique

DESIGNER: Studio Job

www.studiojob.be

Labyrinth

DESIGNER: Studio Job

www.studiojob.be

Belgium / The Netherlands

Perished

DESIGNER: Studio Job

www.studiojob.be

Belgium / The Netherlands

Blood Room

DESIGNER: Studio Job

www.studiojob.be

Invasion Room

DESIGNER: Studio Job

www.studiojob.be

Belgium / The Netherlands

Monastery Room

DESIGNER: Studio Job

www.studiojob.be

A rich land

Boat Room

DESIGNER: Studio Job

www.studiojob.be

Aftermath

DESIGNER: Studio Job

www.studiojob.be

Rugs

DESIGNER: Studio Job

www.studiojob.be

Belgium / The Netherlands

Perished Persian

DESIGNER: Studio Job

www.studiojob.be

Belgium / The Netherlands

Barb Wire

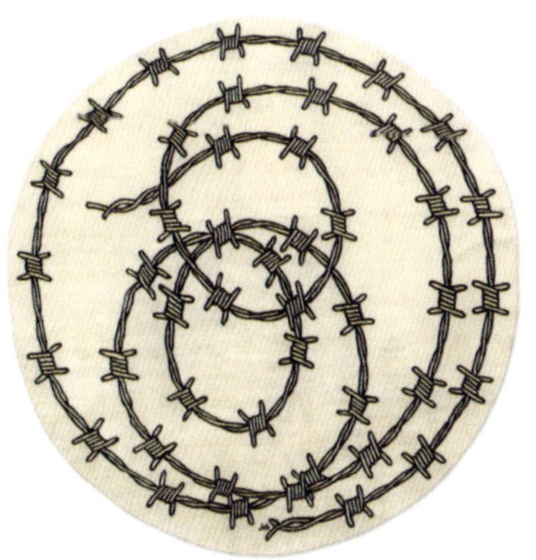

DESIGNER: Studio Job

www.studiojob.be

◂ Symphony

DESIGNER: Studio Job

www.studiojob.be

Viking
▼

Underworld

DESIGNER: Studio Job

www.studiojob.be

Belgium / The Netherlands

Withered Flowers

DESIGNER: Studio Job

www.studiojob.be

Job Suite

DESIGNER: Studio Job

www.studiojob.be

United States

Bacchus & Luxor

DESIGNER: Katie Leede

www.katieleede.com/home/#/Home

William Eggleston's Guide

Ikat

DESIGNER: Katie Leede

www.katieleede.com/home/#/Home

United States

Maharaja

DESIGNER: Katie Leede

www.katieleede.com/home/#/Home

Menna & Shade of Sycamore

DESIGNER: Katie Leede

www.katieleede.com/home/#/Home

Ptah

DESIGNER: Katie Leede

www.katieleede.com/home/#/Home

United States

Isis

DESIGNER: Katie Leede

www.katieleede.com/home/#/Home

Osiris & Thebes

DESIGNER: Katie Leede

www.katieleede.com/home/#/Home

Papyrus

DESIGNER: Katie Leede

www.katieleede.com/home/#/Home

Ra Amun Border

DESIGNER: Katie Leede

www.katieleede.com/home/#/Home

United States

Shade of Sycamore

DESIGNER: Katie Leede

www.katieleede.com/home/#/Home

N-MICHEL FRANK

Spain

Nature

DESIGNER: Estrella Arribas Cabrera

www.estrellaac.com

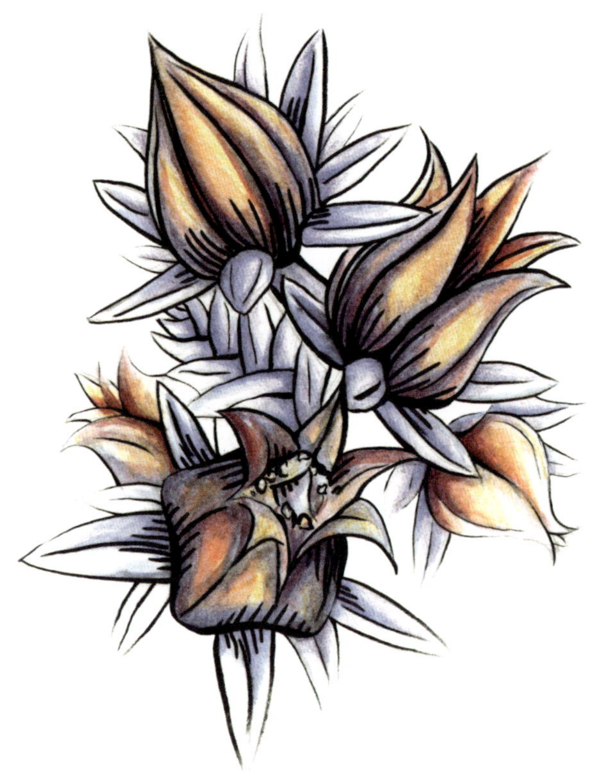

Belarus

Humpty Dumpty

STUDIO: Fajno Design

fajnodesign.by/ru/skills/industrials

Belarus

Children's Room

STUDIO: Fajno Design

fajnodesign.by/ru/skills/industrials

Russia

Mushrooms Pattern

DESIGNER: Juli Puli

www.behance.net/julipuli

Spain

Botany

DESIGNER: Miguel A. Mazon

empatte.com

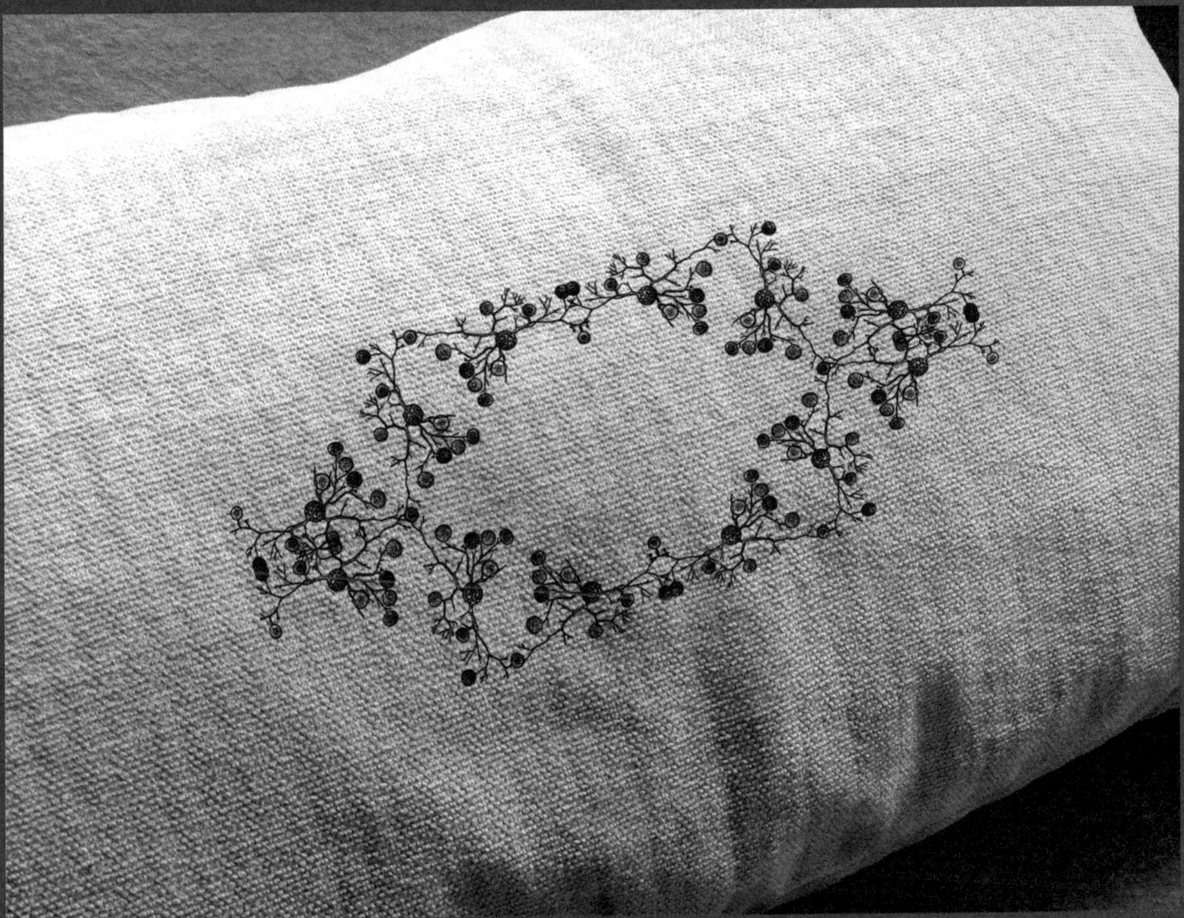

Spain

Botany

DESIGNER: Miguel A. Mazon

empatte.com

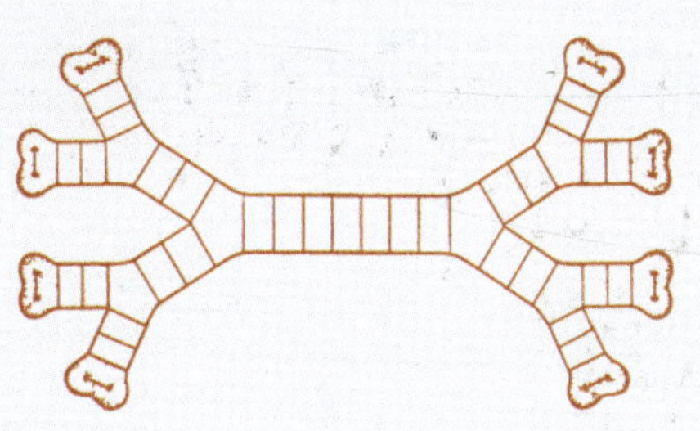

Spain

Diamond

DESIGNER: Miguel A. Mazon

empatte.com

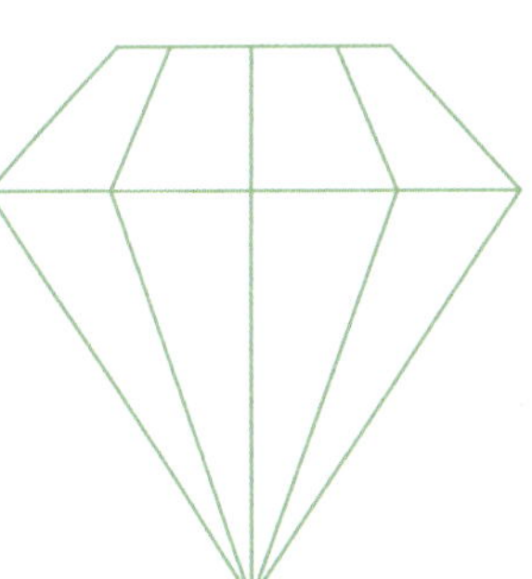

Spain

Farola

DESIGNER: Miguel A. Mazon

empatte.com

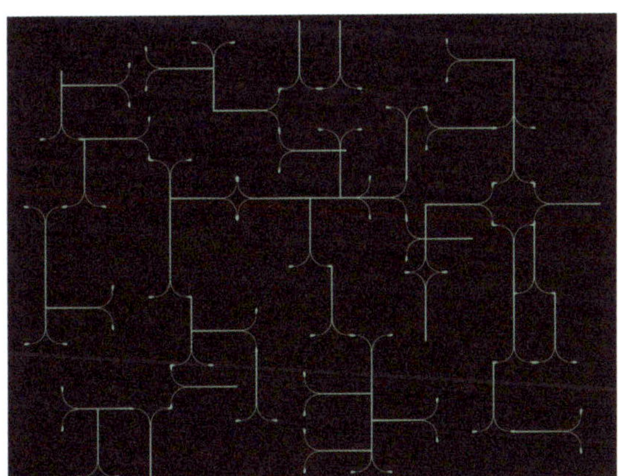

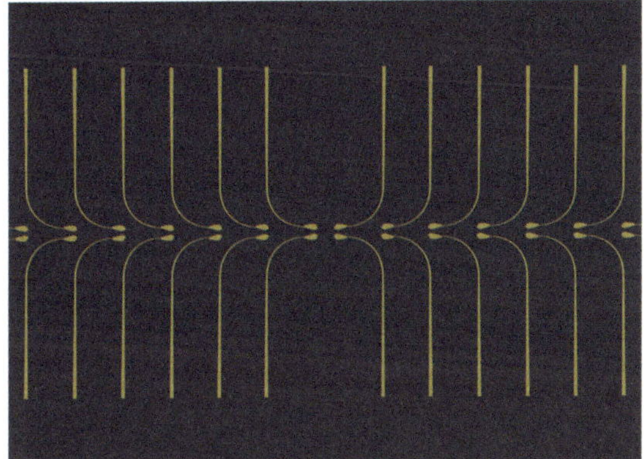

Spain

Trama

DESIGNER: Miguel A. Mazon

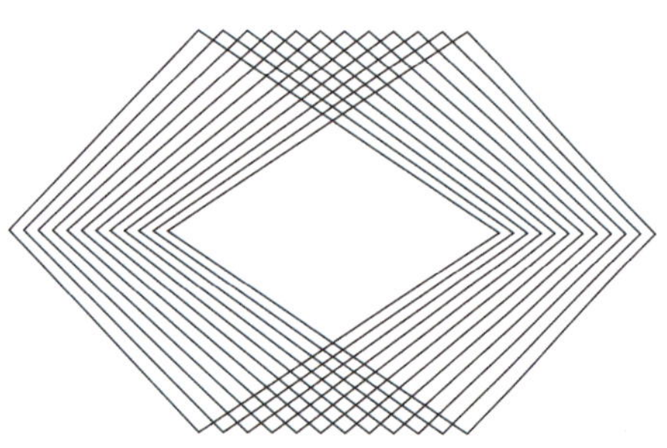

empatte.com

TIKI modern
XXL Living

Italy

The Abstract Nature

Interior and Pictures by Lilly Red Photography

DESIGNER: Sarah Edith

www.behance.net/sarahedith

Interior by LORENA MASDEA Pictures by LUISA VALIERI

South Africa

Paradise is Here

DESIGNER: Heather Moore

skinnylaminx.com

Skinny
laMinx

Skinny
laMinx

Skinny
laMinx

United Kingdom

Make a House a Home

DESIGNER: Ahmad Alameddine

www.alameddinedesign.co.uk

CLOTH
THE LEBANESE KITCHEN

United Kingdom

Aeronaut

STUDIO: Kate Usher Studio

www.kateusher.co.uk

Hang About

STUDIO: Kate Usher Studio

www.kateusher.co.uk

Sharkbait

STUDIO: Kate Usher Studio

www.kateusher.co.uk

United Kingdom

Parasol Parade

STUDIO: Kate Usher Studio

www.kateusher.co.uk

United Kingdom

Oh Sweetie

STUDIO: Kate Usher Studio

www.kateusher.co.uk

United Kingdom

Roll-up

STUDIO: Kate Usher Studio

www.kateusher.co.uk

LADIES AND GENTLEMEN
CHILDREN OF ALL AGES
THE MOST AMAZING AND MARVELOUS MIRACULOUS MENAGERIE
ACROBATIC ACTS
OUTRAGEOUSLY ASTONISHING
STEP INSIDE OUR DAZZLING BIG TOP
ADMIT ONE

Turtle

STUDIO: Kate Usher Studio

www.kateusher.co.uk

United Kingdom

Mr Meerkat

STUDIO: Kate Usher Studio

www.kateusher.co.uk

Finland

Älgört

CLIENT: Ikea of Sweden
DESIGNER: Niina Aalto, Emma Hagman, Pinja Laine

www.studiokelkka.com/en

◂ Ängsspira

DESIGNER: Niina Aalto, Pinja Laine

DESIGNER: Emma Hagman, Niina Aalto

Gulört Cushion

▾

CLIENT: Ikea of Sweden

STUDIO: Studio Kelkka

www.studiokelkka.com/en

◂ Älgört

DESIGNER: Niina Aalto

Gulört Cushion Cover ▸

DESIGNER: Niina Aalto, Pinja Laine, Linda Svarfvar

DESIGNER: Niina Aalto

Gulört Rug

▾

▲
Lyndby

DESIGNER: Niina Aalto

◂ Halvlop

DESIGNER: Pinja Laine

CLIENT: Ikea of Sweden
STUDIO: Studio Kelkka

www.studiokelkka.com/en

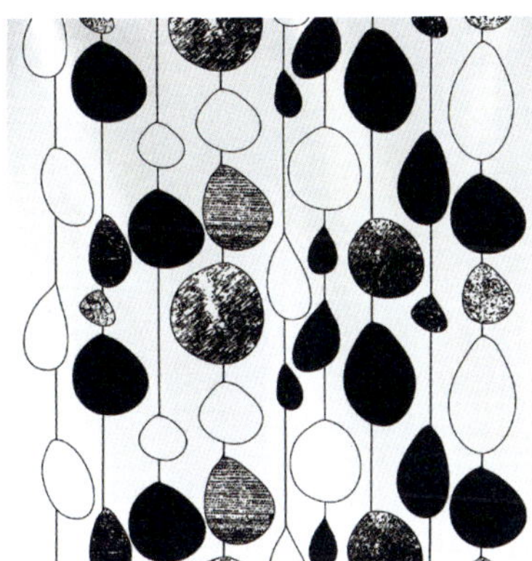

▲
Bollkaktus

DESIGNER: Henna Jaakkola

▲
Tydingen

DESIGNER: Niina Aalto

▲
Langrör

DESIGNER: Niina Aalto

Färgkulla

CLIENT: Ikea of Sweden
STUDIO: Studio Kelkka
DESIGNER: Niina Aalto

www.studiokelkka.com/en

Kajsamia

CLIENT: Ikea of Sweden
STUDIO: Studio Kelkka
DESIGNER: Emma Hagman

www.studiokelkka.com/en

Malin Rund

CLIENT: Ikea of Sweden
STUDIO: Studio Kelkka
DESIGNER: Niina Aalto

www.studiokelkka.com/en

Finland

Malin Löv

CLIENT: Ikea of Sweden
STUDIO: Studio Kelkka
DESIGNER:Eivor Fågel, Malin Löv

www.studiokelkka.com/en

Finland

Eivor Fågel

CLIENT: Ikea of Sweden
STUDIO: Studio Kelkka
DESIGNER: Niina Aalto

www.studiokelkka.com/en

Finland

Black & White–REPETERA Collection

CLIENT: Ikea of Sweden
STUDIO: Studio Kelkka
DESIGNER: Salla Tervonen

www.studiokelkka.com

Finland

The Leaves–REPETERA Collection

CLIENT: Ikea of Sweden
STUDIO: Studio Kelkka
DESIGNER: Pinja Laine

www.studiokelkka.com

Finland

The Innocent World–REPETERA Collection

CLIENT: Ikea of Sweden
STUDIO: Studio Kelkka
DESIGNER: Towels – Niina Aalto, Emma Hagman; Bathroom mat – Emma Hagman; Shower curtain – Niina Aalto, Salla Tervonen

www.studiokelkka.com

Finland

Nature–REPETERA Collection

CLIENT: Ikea of Sweden
STUDIO: Studio Kelkka
DESIGNERS: Emma Hagman, Susanna Hoikkala, Salla Tervonen

www.studiokelkka.com

Finland

Knitted Leaves

CLIENT: Wallunica
STUDIO: Studio Kelkka
DESIGNER: Emma Hagman

www.studiokelkka.com

Finland

Paris Flower

CLIENT: Wallunica
STUDIO: Studio Kelkka
DESIGNER: Salla Tervonen

www.studiokelkka.com

Finland

Heinä

CLIENT: Wallunica
STUDIO: Studio Kelkka
DESIGNER: Terhi Laine

www.studiokelkka.com

Finland

Imarre

CLIENT: Wallunica
STUDIO: Studio Kelkka
DESIGNER: Kirsi Sundell

www.studiokelkka.com

Blossom

CLIENT: Wallunica
STUDIO: Studio Kelkka
DESIGNER: Henna Jaakkola

www.studiokelkka.com

Finland

Capsula

CLIENT: Wallunica
STUDIO: Studio Kelkka
DESIGNER: Linda Svarfvar

www.studiokelkka.com

Finland

Chlorophyll

CLIENT: Wallunica
STUDIO: Studio Kelkka
DESIGNER: Ulla Lapiolahti

www.studiokelkka.com

Finland

Herbarium

CLIENT: Wallunica
STUDIO: Studio Kelkka
DESIGNER: Niina Aalto

www.studiokelkka.com

Finland

Fields

CLIENT: Wallunica
STUDIO: Studio Kelkka
DESIGNER: Susanna Hoikkala

www.studiokelkka.com

Finland

Fir Tree

CLIENT: Wallunica
STUDIO: Studio Kelkka
DESIGNER: Pinja Laine

www.studiokelkka.com

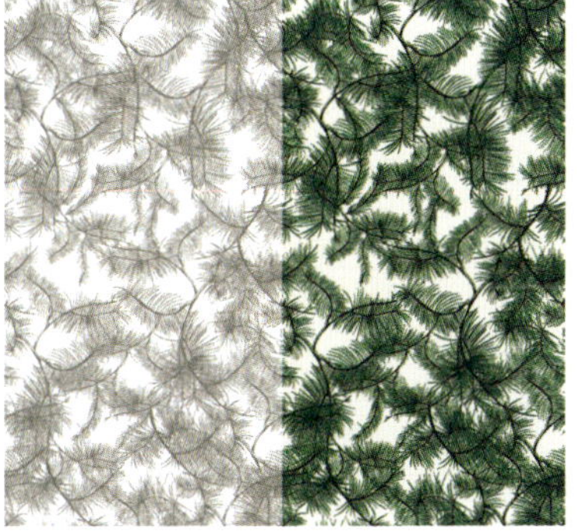

Sweden

Coco Tiger

STUDIO: Studio Lisa Bengtsson
DESIGNER: Lisa Bengtsson

www.studiolisabengtsson.com

Sweden

Go Bananas

STUDIO: Studio Lisa Bengtsson
DESIGNER: Lisa Bengtsson

www.studiolisabengtsson.com

Tillsammans

STUDIO: Studio Lisa Bengtsson
DESIGNER: Lisa Bengtsson

www.studiolisabengtsson.com

United States

Happy Daisies

DESIGNER: Emily Roberson Wallace

society6.com/southernemma

United States

Lucky Umbrellas

DESIGNER: Emily Roberson Wallace

society6.com/southernemma

United States

Wispy Flowers

DESIGNER: Emily Wallace

www.behance.net/gallery/20855383/New-Floral-Patterns-Oct-2014

Spain

Acapulco

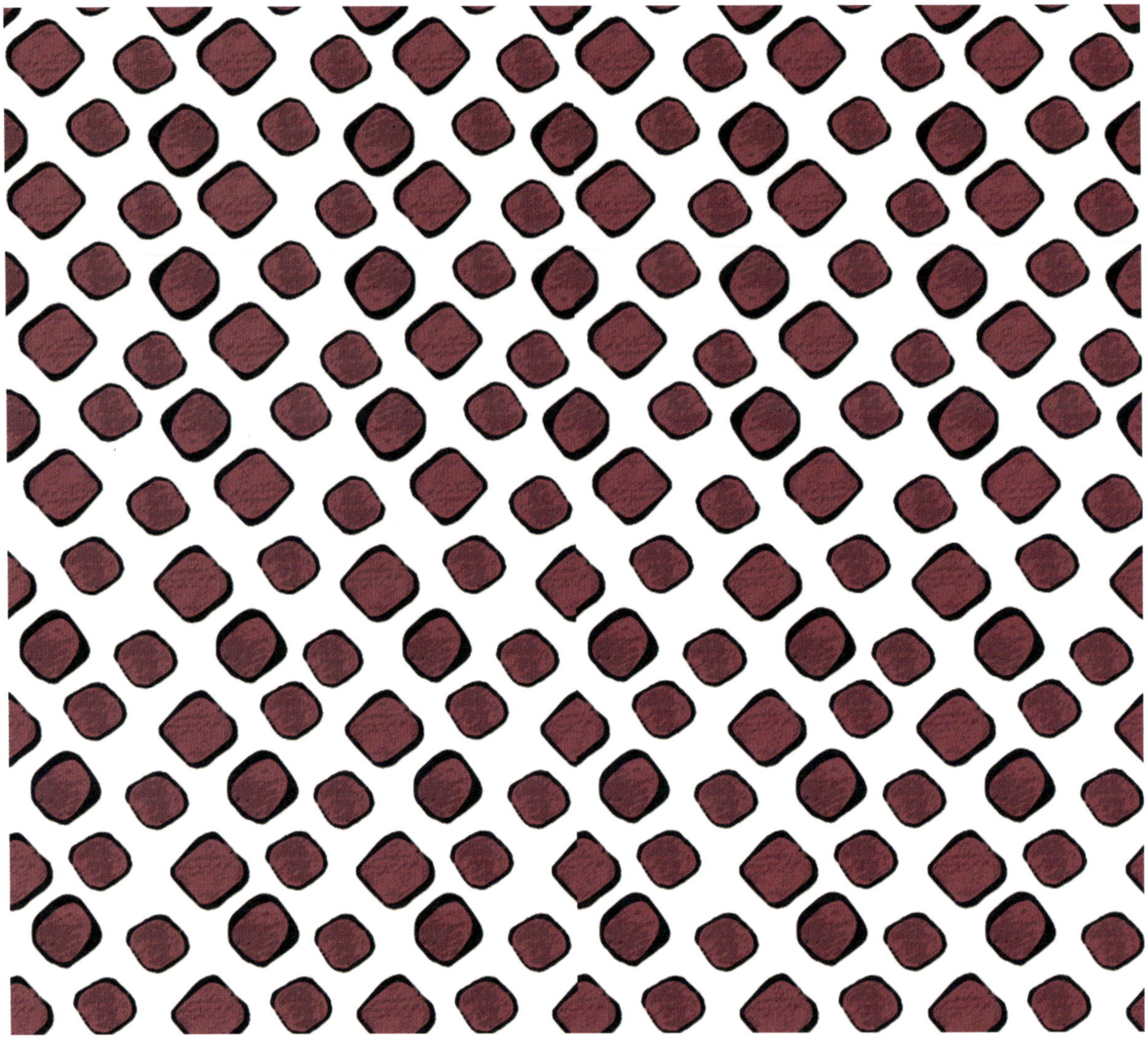

STUDIO: The Bartl Studio
DESIGNER: Cristina R. Bartl Villa

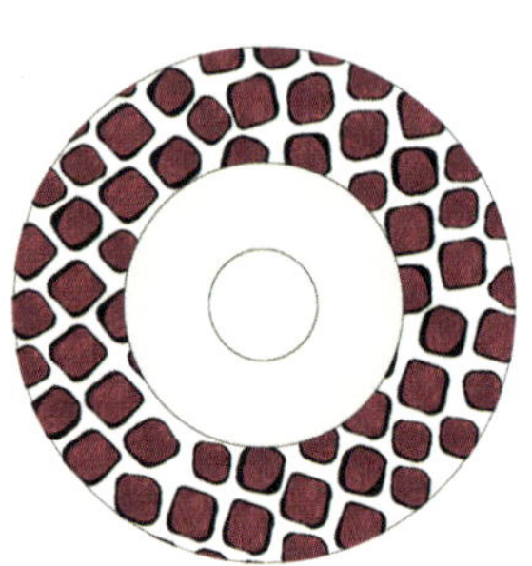

thebartlstudio.com

Spain

Lobsters

STUDIO: The Bartl Studio

DESIGNER: Cristina R. Bartl Villa

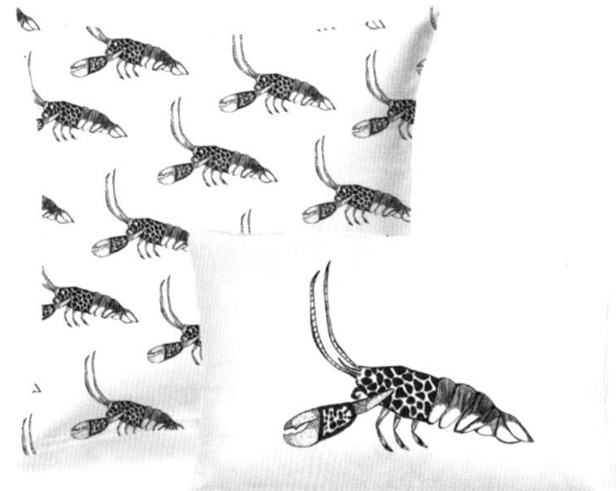

thebartlstudio.com

Night in Manhattan

STUDIO: The Bartl Studio
DESIGNER: Cristina R. Bartl Villa

thebartlstudio.com

Spain

English Garden

STUDIO: The Bartl Studio
DESIGNER: Cristina R. Bartl Villa

thebartlstudio.com

Cats

STUDIO: The Bartl Studio
DESIGNER: Cristina R. Bartl Villa

thebartlstudio.com

Spain

Sailing in Majorca

STUDIO: The Bartl Studio
DESIGNER: Cristina R. Bartl Villa

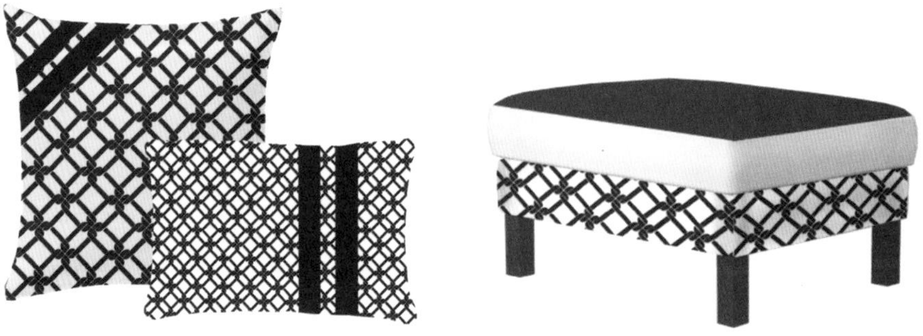

thebartlstudio.com

Spain

Bears

STUDIO: The Bartl Studio
DESIGNER: Cristina R. Bartl Villa

thebartlstudio.com

Spain

Fruit Punch

STUDIO: The Bartl Studio
DESIGNER: Cristina R. Bartl Villa

thebartlstudio.com

Spain

Fairies & Cupcakes

STUDIO: The Bartl Studio
DESIGNER: Cristina R. Bartl Villa

thebartlstudio.com

Spain

Butterflies

STUDIO: The Bartl Studio
DESIGNER: Cristina R. Bartl Villa

thebartlstudio.com

Orders

STUDIO: Royal Design Studio

www.royaldesignstudio.com

Grace

STUDIO: Royal Design Studio

www.royaldesignstudio.com

African Protea Allover

STUDIO: Royal Design Studio

www.royaldesignstudio.com

United States

Elegance

STUDIO: Royal Design Studio

www.royaldesignstudio.com

Large Atlas Allover

STUDIO: Royal Design Studio

www.royaldesignstudio.com

United States

Dot Dot Dot

STUDIO: Royal Design Studio

www.royaldesignstudio.com

Large Kinetic Floral

STUDIO: Royal Design Studio

www.royaldesignstudio.com

United States

Tribal Vibe Allover

STUDIO: Royal Design Studio

www.royaldesignstudio.com

United States

Herringbone Shuffle

STUDIO: Royal Design Studio

www.royaldesignstudio.com

United States

Deco Diamonds

STUDIO: Royal Design Studio

www.royaldesignstudio.com

United States

Annapakshi Indian Damask

STUDIO: Royal Design Studio

www.royaldesignstudio.com

United States

Daisy Dot

STUDIO: Royal Design Studio

www.royaldesignstudio.com

Bloomers

STUDIO: Royal Design Studio

www.royaldesignstudio.com

Herringbone

STUDIO: Royal Design Studio

www.royaldesignstudio.com

Tribal Batik

STUDIO: Royal Design Studio

www.royaldesignstudio.com

United States

Otomi Allover Damask & Talavera

STUDIO: Royal Design Studio

www.royaldesignstudio.com

Otomi Allover Damask & Talavera

STUDIO: Royal Design Studio

www.royaldesignstudio.com

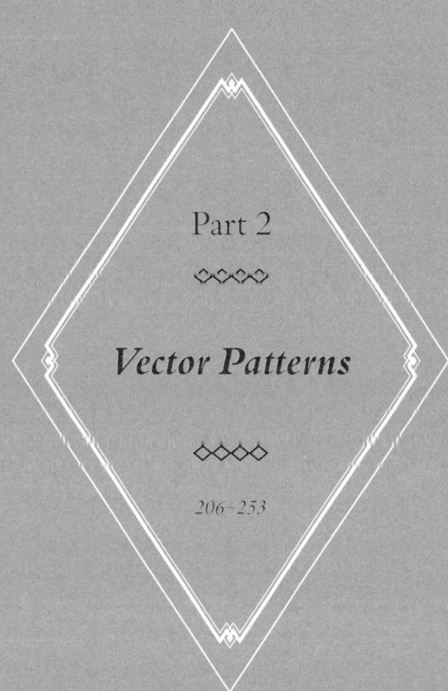

Part 2

Vector Patterns

206~253

1/2

3/4

5/6

7

8/9

10/11

12

13/14

15

16/17

18

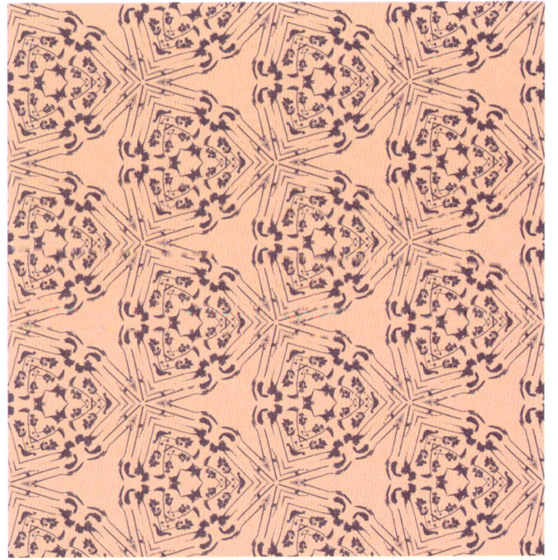

19/20

21

22

23/24

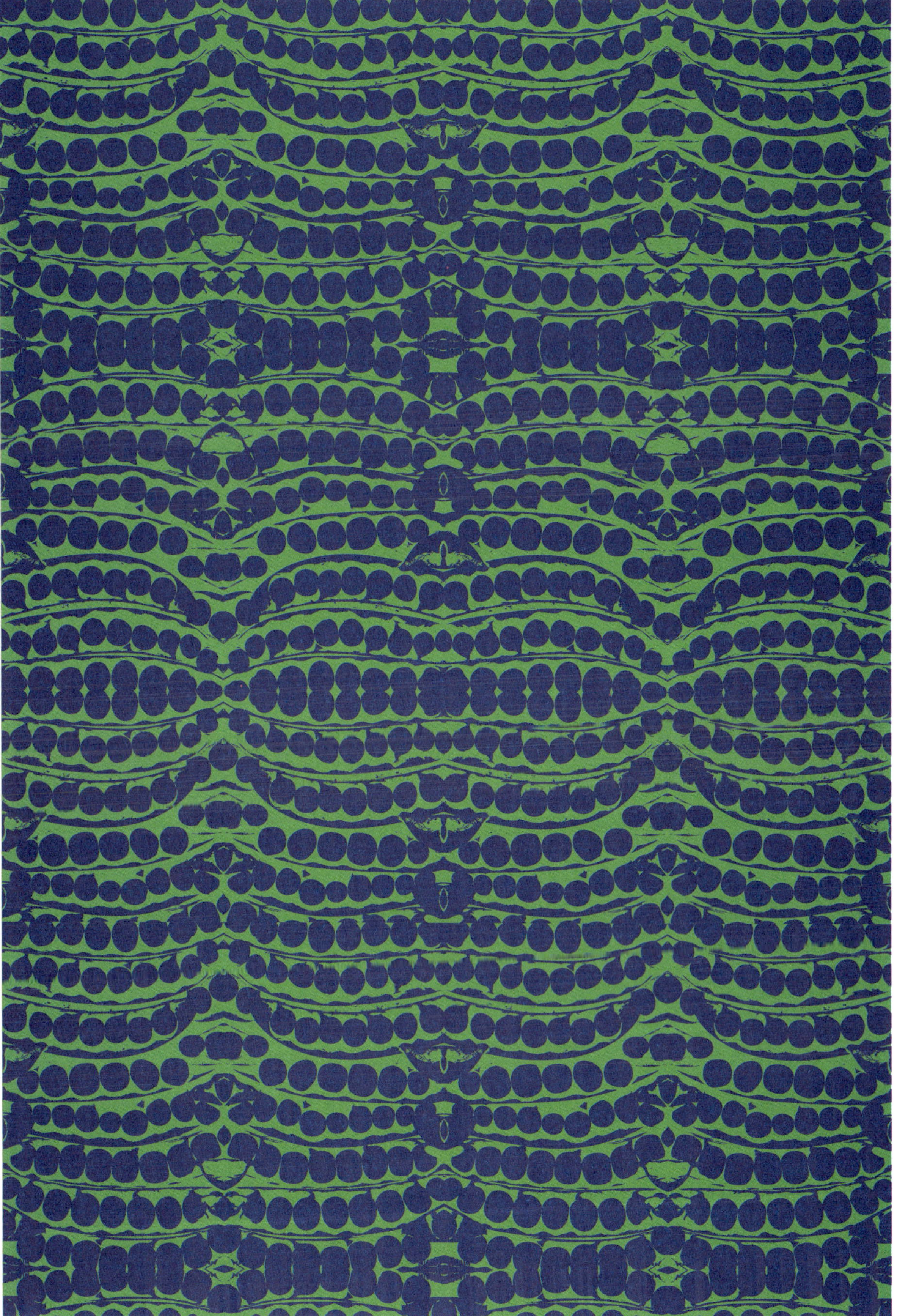

26

27

28

29

30/31

32

33/34

35

36

37/38
39/40
41/42

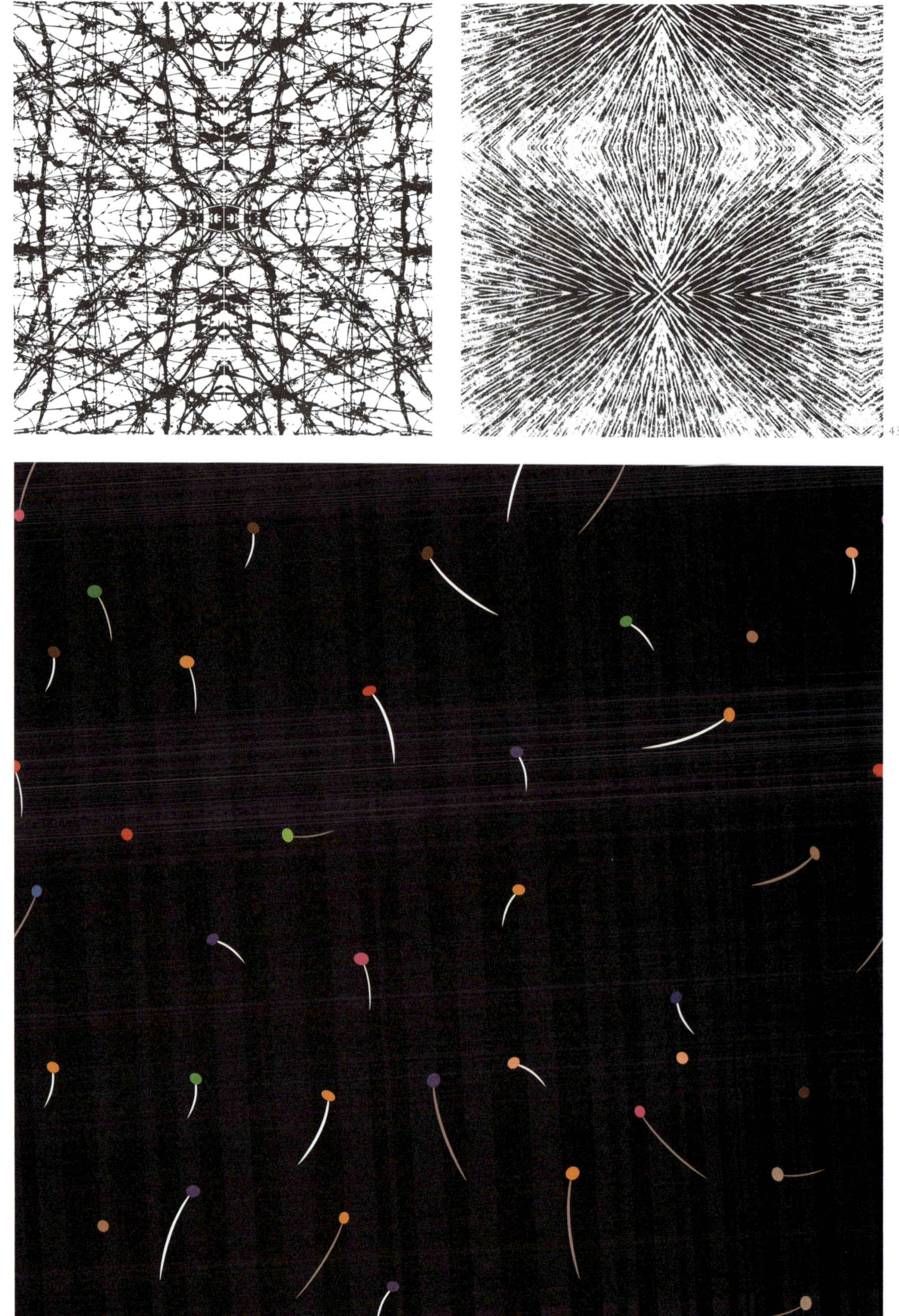

43/44

45

46/47

48

49/50

51

52/53

54

55/56

57/58

59/60

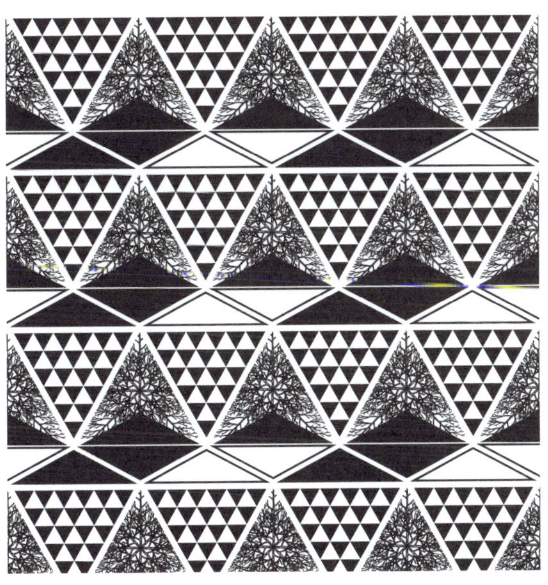

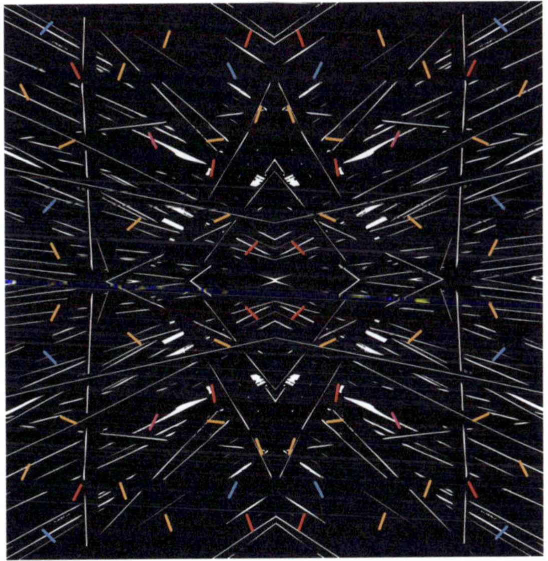

61/62

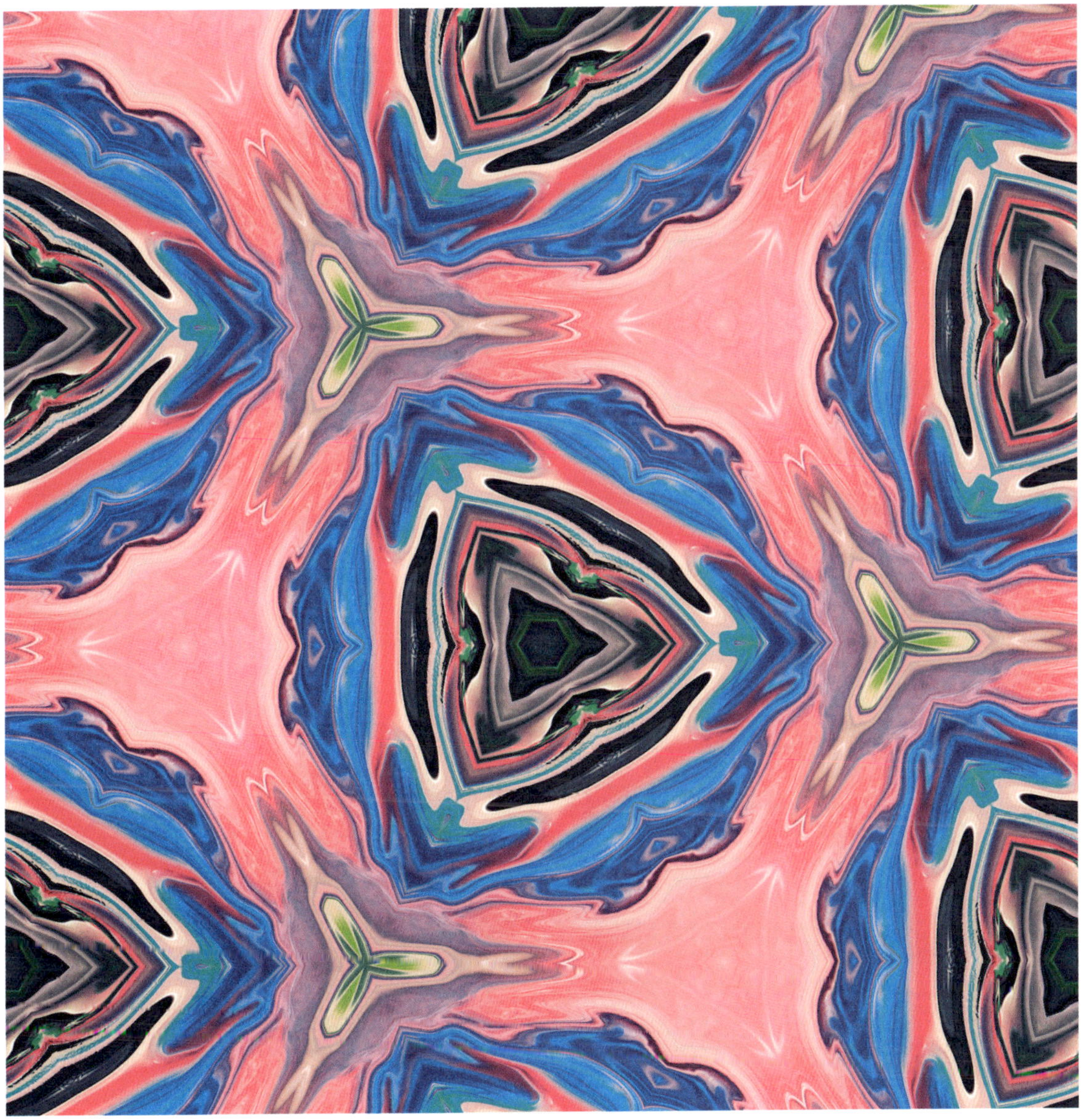

63

64/65

66

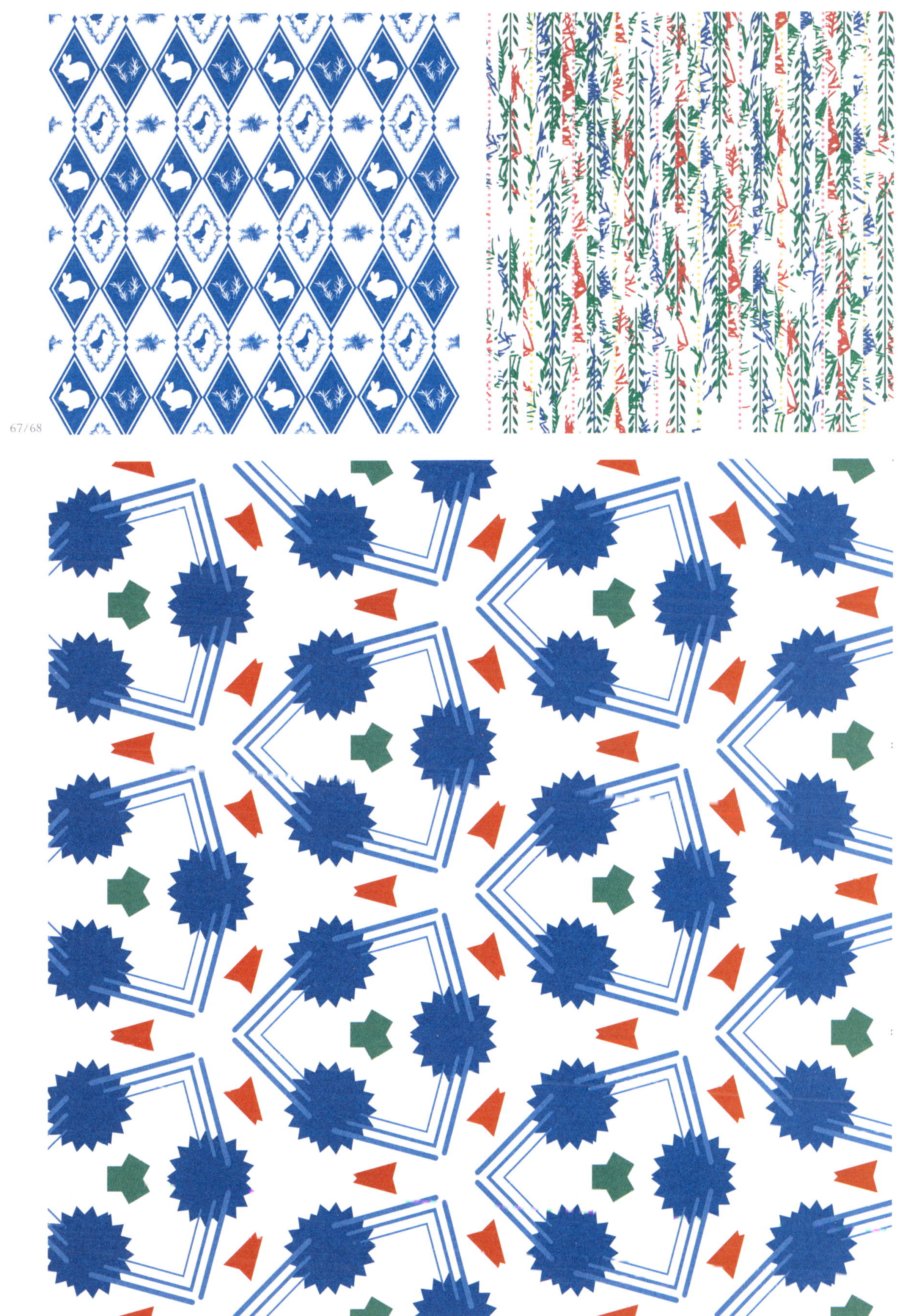

67/68

69

70/71

72

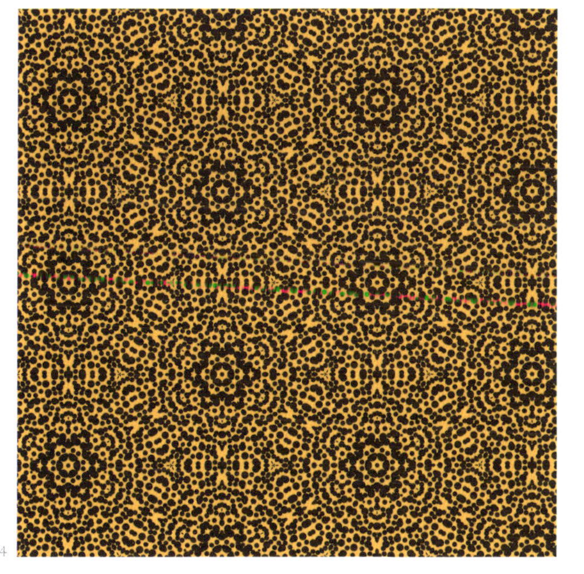

73/74

75

76/77

78/79

80/81

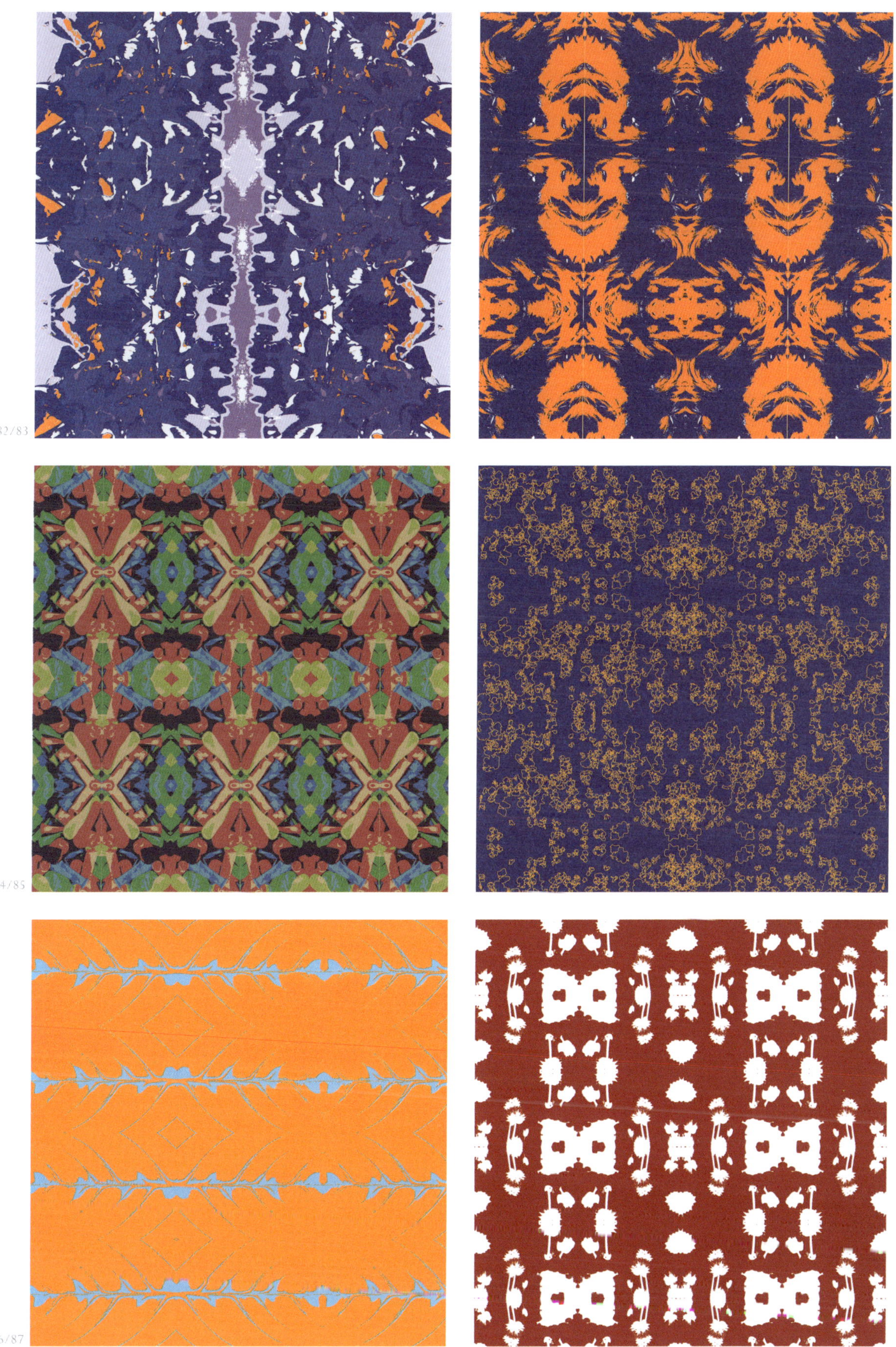
82/83
84/85
86/87

88/89

90/91

92/93

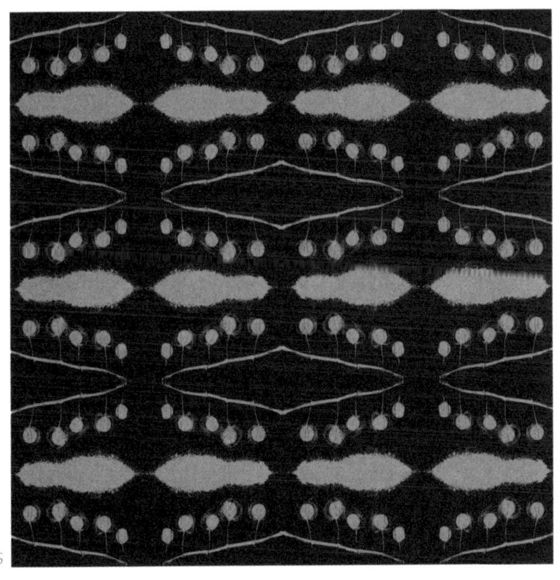

94/95

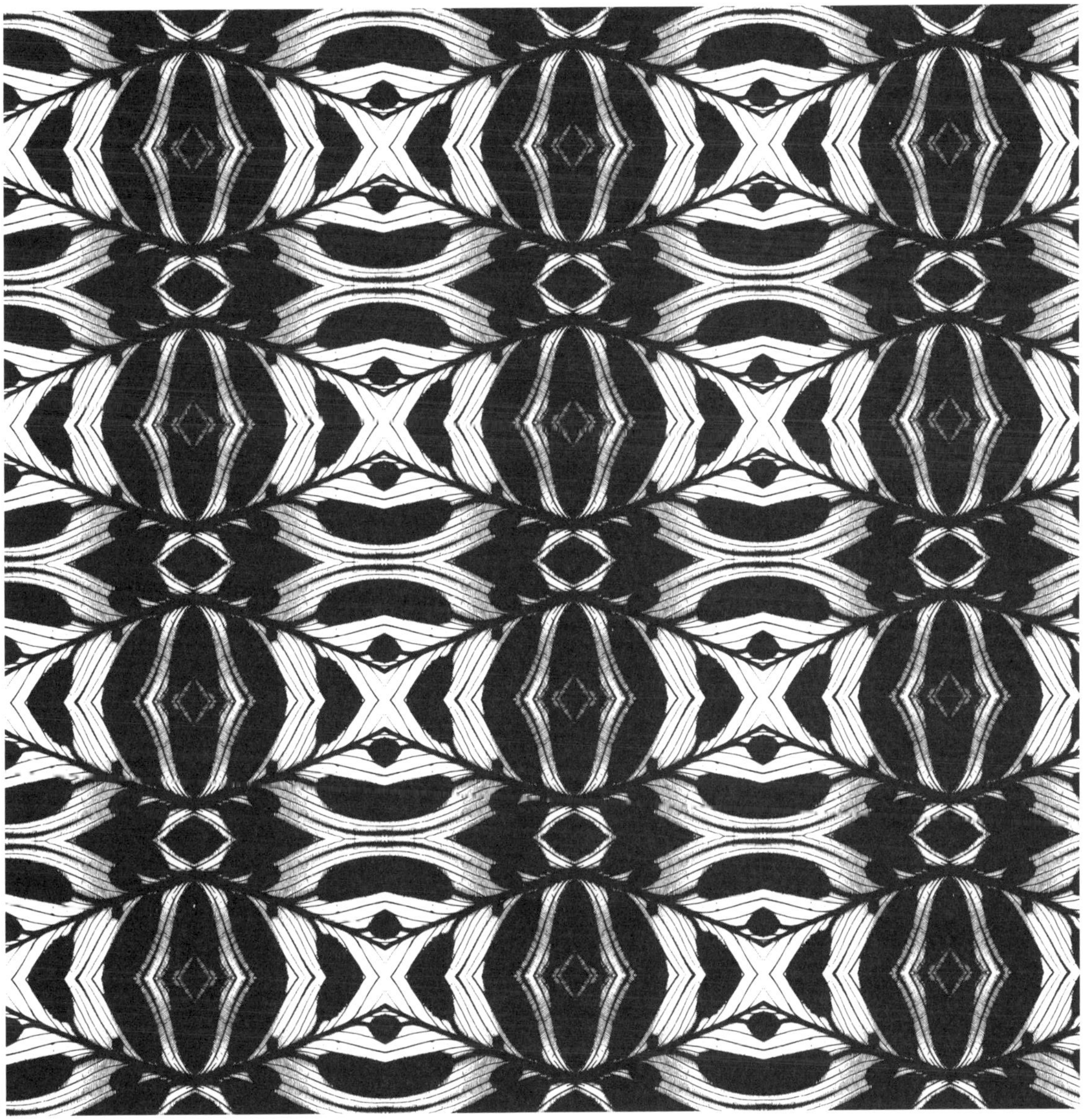

96

97/98

99/100

101/102

103/104

105/106

107/108

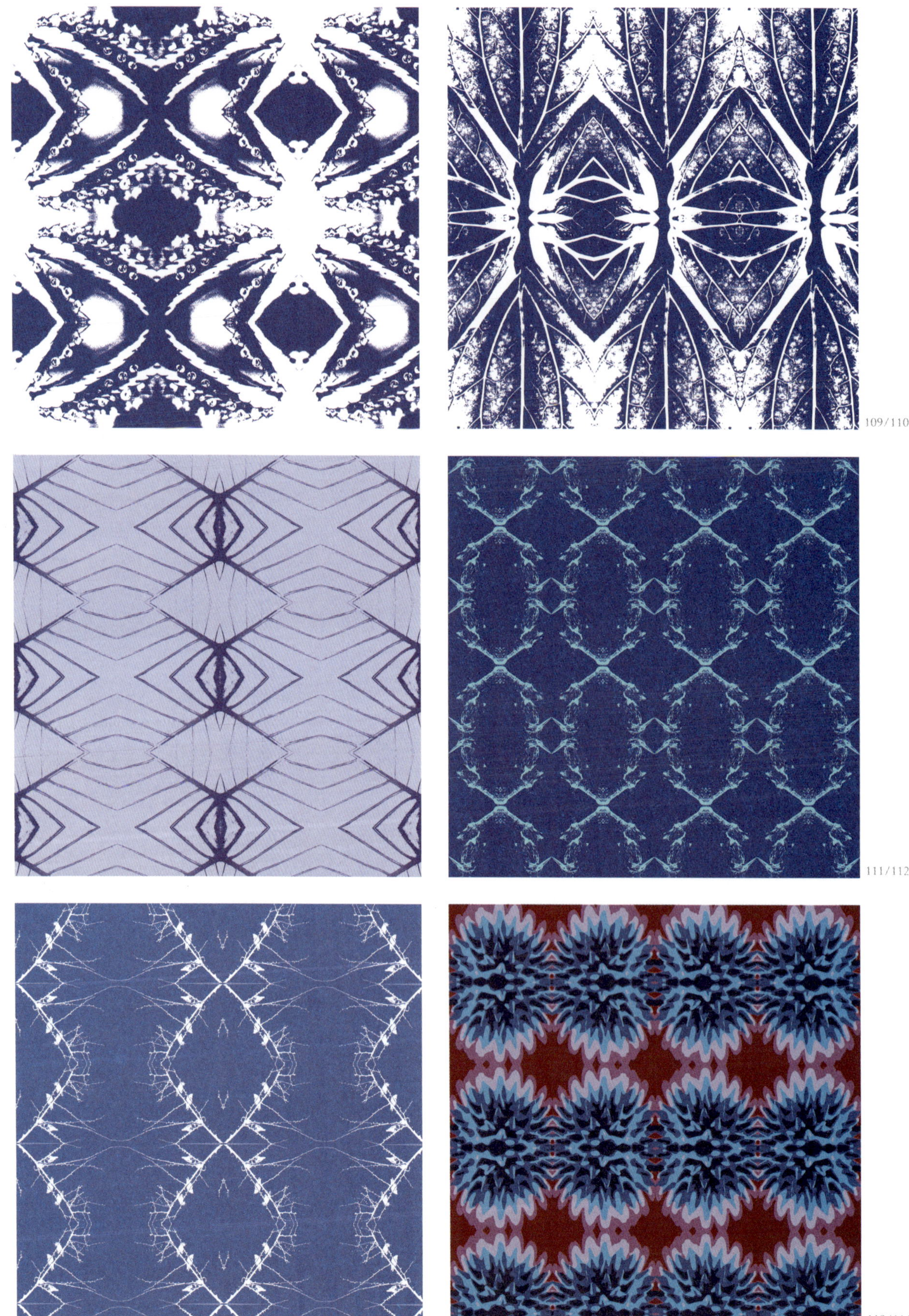

109/110

111/112

113/114

115/116

117

118

119/120

121/122

123/124

125/126

127

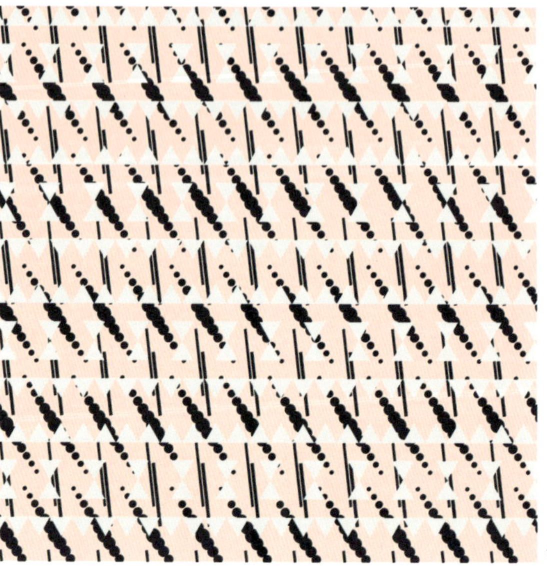

128/129

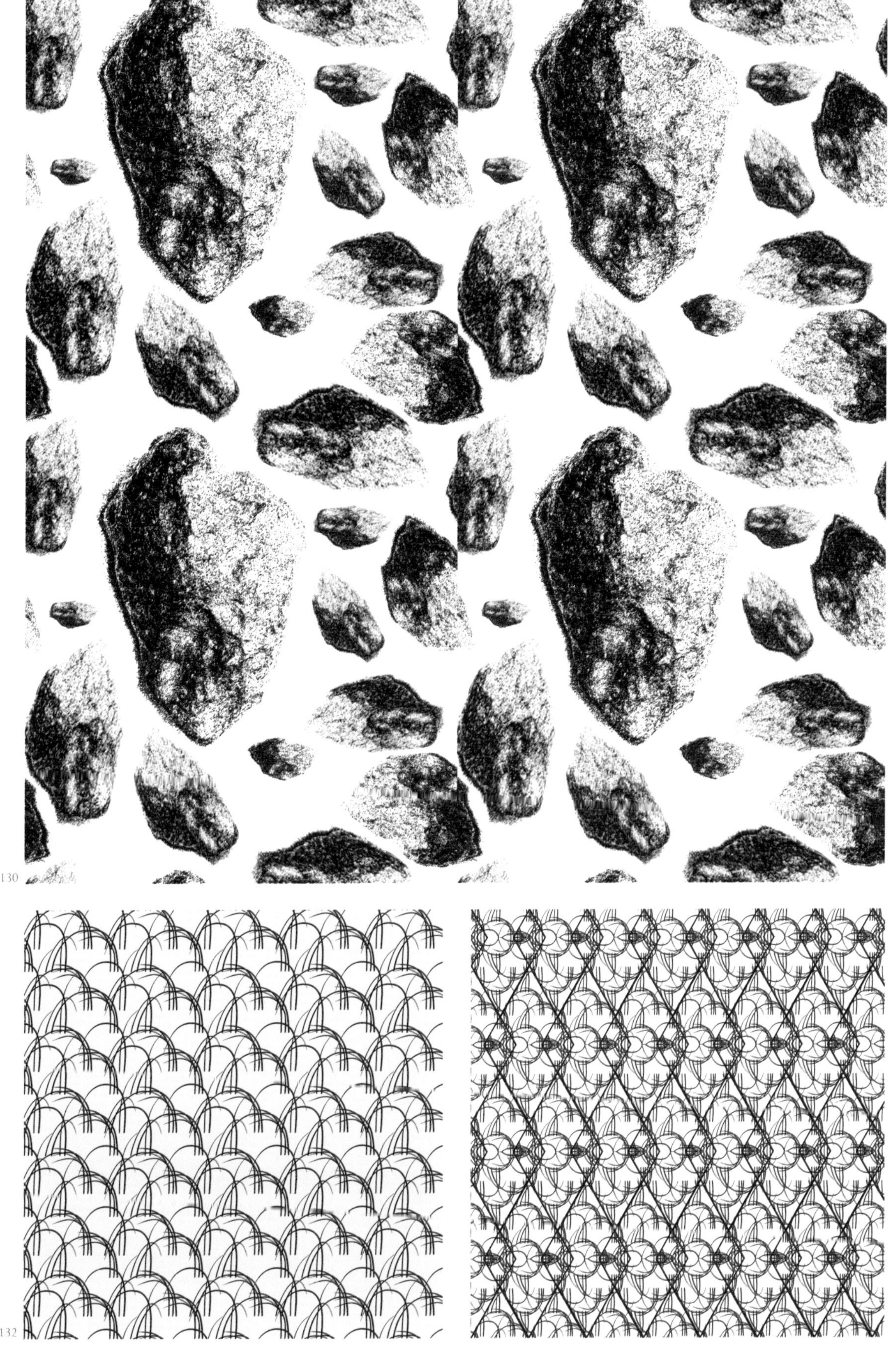

130

131/132

133/134

135/136

137/138

139/140

141/142

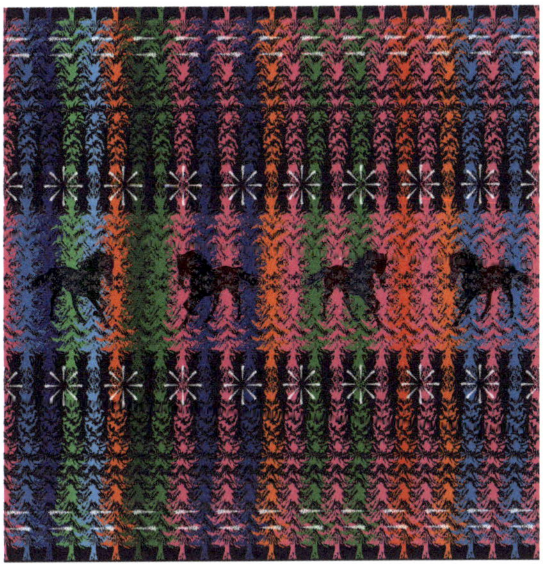
143/144

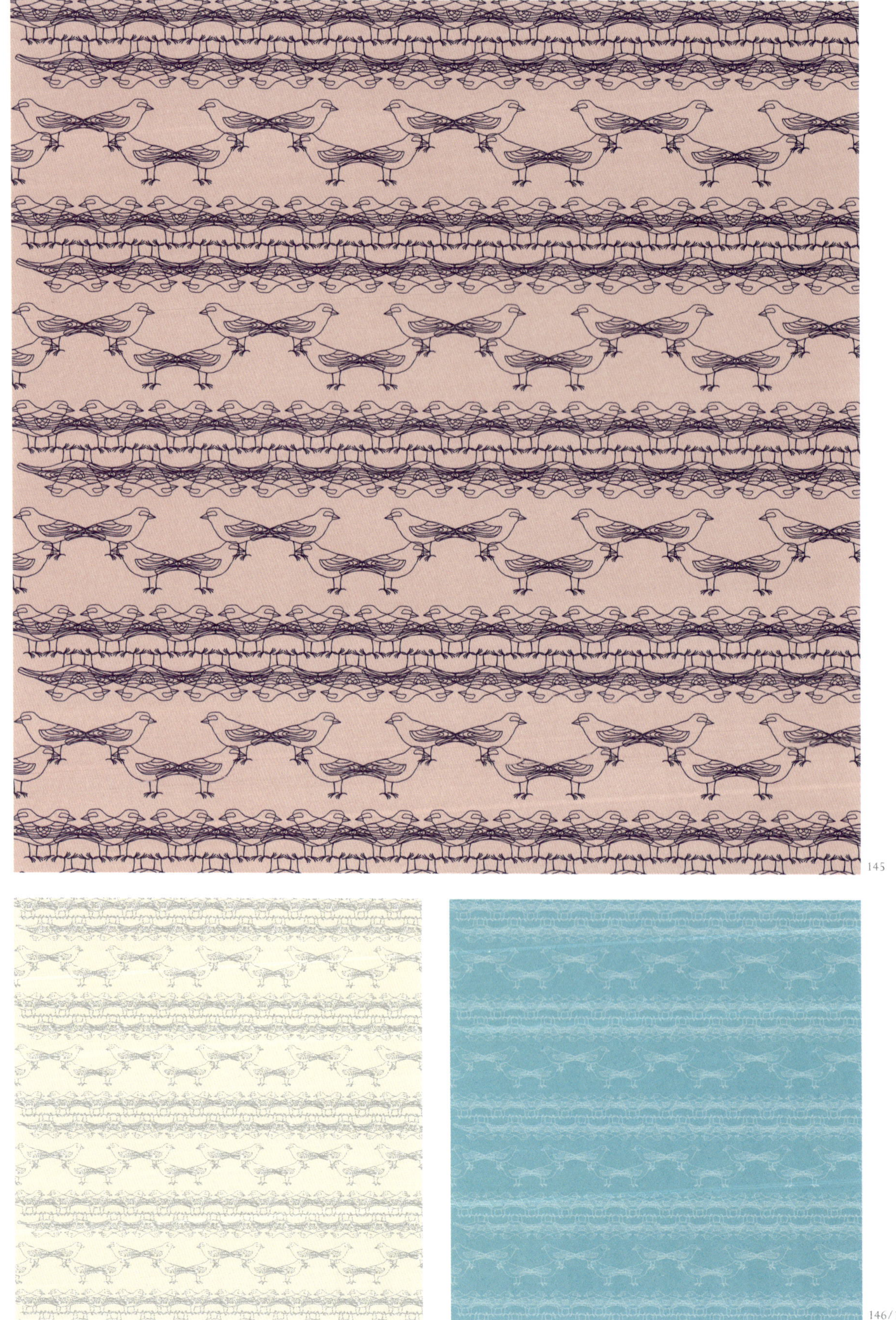

145

146/147

148

149/150

151/152

153/154

155/156

157/158

159/160

161/162

163

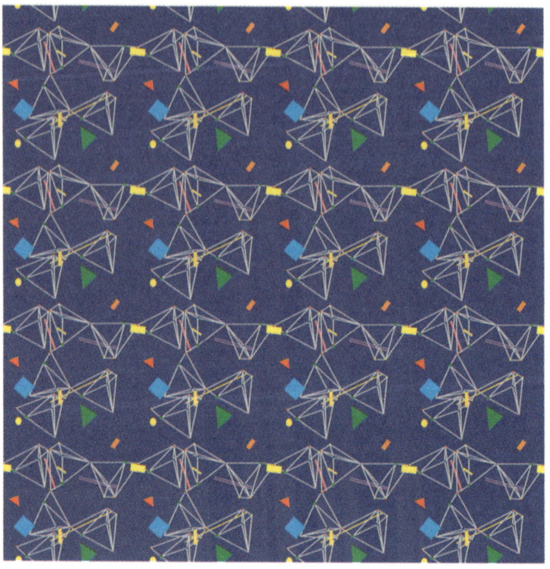

164/165

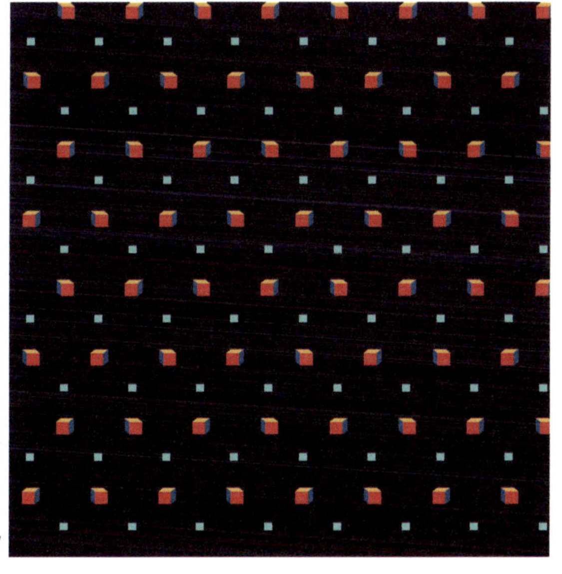

166/167

168

169/170

171/172

173/174

175/176

177/178

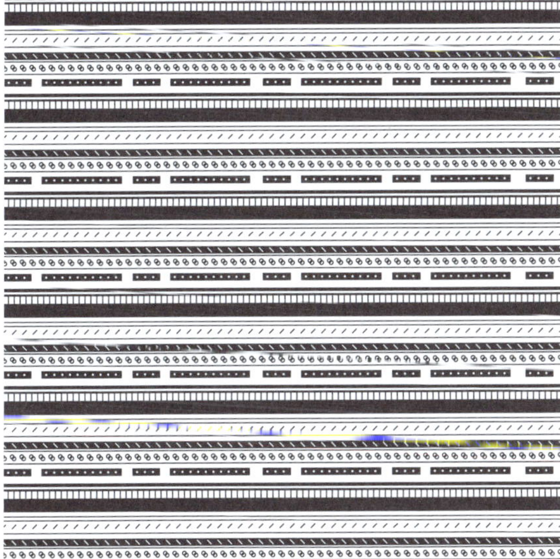

179/180

Index

ACKNOWLEDGEMENTS

We would like to thank all the designers and contributers who have been involved in the production of this book. Their contribution is indispensable in the compilation of this book. We would also like to express our gratitude to all the producers for their invaluable opinions and assistance throughout this project. And to the many others whose names are not credited but have aided in the production of this book, we thank you for your continuous support.

FUTURE COOPERATIONS: If you wish to participate in SendPoints' future projects and publications, please send your website or portfolio to editor01@sendpoints.cn